Little Mitchie

LET'S LOOK INSIDE A RABBIT'S BURROW

LET'S LOOK INSIDE: ANIMAL HOMES

TRACY VONDER BRINK

CREATING YOUNG NONFICTION READERS

Little Mitchie books spark curiosity and support early nonfiction reading for students in Grades 2-3. Designed to build vocabulary, support second language learners, and prepare readers for middle-grade content, each book includes helpful tips for parents and educators to build confidence and deepen understanding of the world.

TIPS FOR READING NONFICTION WITH BEGINNING READERS

Talk about Nonfiction

Begin by explaining that nonfiction books give us information that is true. The book will be organized around a specific topic or idea, and we may learn new facts through reading.

Look at the Parts

Most nonfiction books have helpful features. Our *Little Mitchie* titles include color photographs and graphic aids, a table of contents, a glossary, and an index. Share the purpose of these features with your reader.

Color Photos and Graphic Aids

A lot of information can be found by "reading" photos, charts, maps, and other graphic aids found within nonfiction texts. Help your reader learn more about the different ways information can be displayed.

Table of Contents

Located at the front of the book, this list shows the big ideas within the text and the page numbers where they can be found.

Glossary

Located at the back of the book, the glossary defines key words and phrases that are related to the topic. These words and phrases can be found in the text in colored type.

Index

Located at the back of the book, an index is an alphabetical list of topics and the page numbers where they can be found.

With a little help and guidance about reading nonfiction, you can feel good about introducing a young reader to the world of *Little Mitchie* nonfiction books.

Little Mitchie is an imprint of:

Mitchell Lane
PUBLISHERS

2001 SW 31st Avenue
Hallandale, FL 33009
mitchelllanepub.com

First Edition, 2027.

Author: Tracy Vonder Brink
Designer: Jen Bowers
Editor: Tricia Hoffman

Library of Congress Cataloging-in-Publication Data
Title: Let's Look Inside a Rabbit's Burrow / by Tracy Vonder Brink

Description: Hallandale, FL : Mitchell Lane Publishers, [2027]

Identifiers:
ISBN 979-8-89260-875-6 (library bound)
ISBN 979-8-89260-972-2 (eBook)

Library of Congress Control Number: 2026936348

PHOTO CREDITS
Shutterstock: cover, p.1 ©2021 Paul Abrahams, p.5 ©2015 Rudmer Zwerver, p.6–7 ©2021 RudiErnst, p.9 ©2020 Fotorina, p.11 ©2023 eliscora, p.13 ©2019 Formatoriginal, p. 14–15 ©2018 Ilkka Koivula, p.17 ©2024 imageBROKER.com, p.18 ©2018 guentermanaus, p.20–21 ©2017 LFRabanedo, p.22 ©StockSmartStart

TABLE OF CONTENTS

Chapter One

REMARKABLE RABBITS

A European rabbit hops out of its underground **burrow**. What was it doing in there? What's life like inside?

HOME SWEET HOME

Not all rabbits dig burrows. Cottontail rabbits live out in the open and take shelter in bushes, tall grass, and sometimes empty burrows dug by other animals.

European rabbits live together in a **colony**. A colony's group of connected burrows is called a warren. Warrens can be 9 feet (3 m) deep and 148 feet (45 m) long.

Chapter Two

PARTS OF A RABBIT WARREN

Warrens have more than one entrance in case the rabbits need to escape fast. They hide the entrances under bushes or rocks. The females do most of the digging.

HOME SWEET HOME

Rabbits thump their back feet to warn that danger is near. Any rabbit that hears the thumping runs to the warren to hide.

The warren's entrances connect to tunnels that end in **chambers**. The tunnels and chambers give the rabbits a place to hide. They also live there. Some chambers are for sleeping. When females are ready to have babies, called kits, they dig **nursery** chambers. They line the nursery with fur and grass to keep the kits warm.

HOME SWEET HOME

To keep her newborn kits safe from **predators**, the female seals up the nursery chamber and only visits long enough to feed them.

Chapter Three

LIFE INSIDE THE WARREN

Rabbits rest in the warren during the day. They come out in the late afternoon or early evening. They stay up all night to look for food and eat.

HOME SWEET HOME

European rabbits gobble grasses, roots, leaves, and other plant parts. They look for food near the warren in case they have to hide from predators.

One warren usually has six to 10 adults and their young. One male and one female are **dominant** over the rest. The top male patrols his **territory** outside the warren. He chases off any males that try to challenge him.

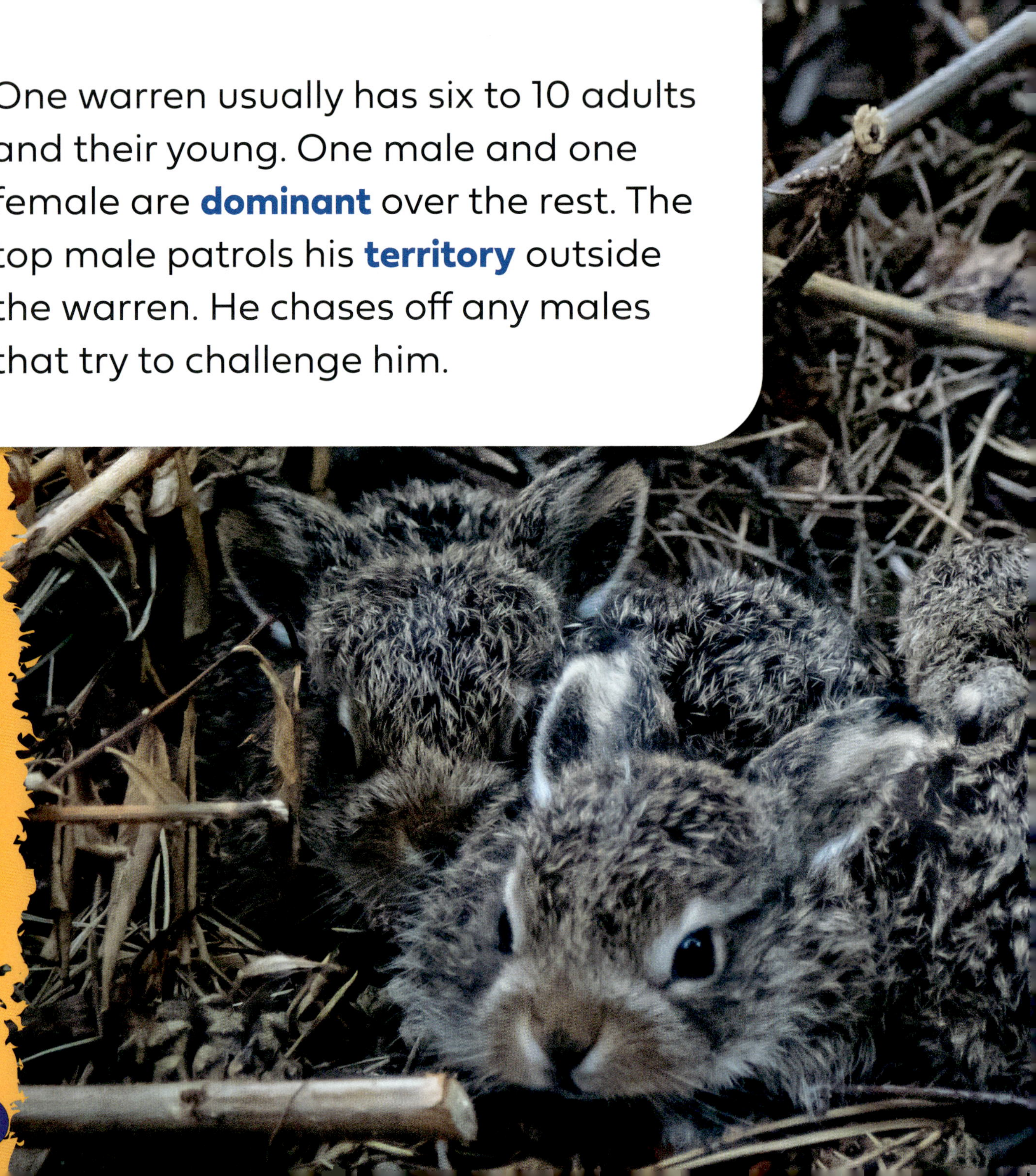

Rabbits know each other by their smell. The top male marks his territory outside by rubbing his chin on rocks and sticks to leave his smell behind. He marks parts of the warren the same way. His smell tells the rest of the colony the warren is home and makes them feel safe. The top male also rubs his chin on rabbits that belong to his colony.

HOME SWEET HOME

Females also chin mark. They rub their chins on their kits so the babies smell like part of the colony.

Rabbits poop and pee outside the warren. They dig out **shallow** areas on the ground and always go in the same spots. Going outside not only keeps the warren clean but also tells other rabbits whose territory it is.

A warren gives rabbits a place to rest and hide from predators. It's also a safe place to have their young. Now you know what life is like in a rabbit's burrow!

A LOOK INSIDE

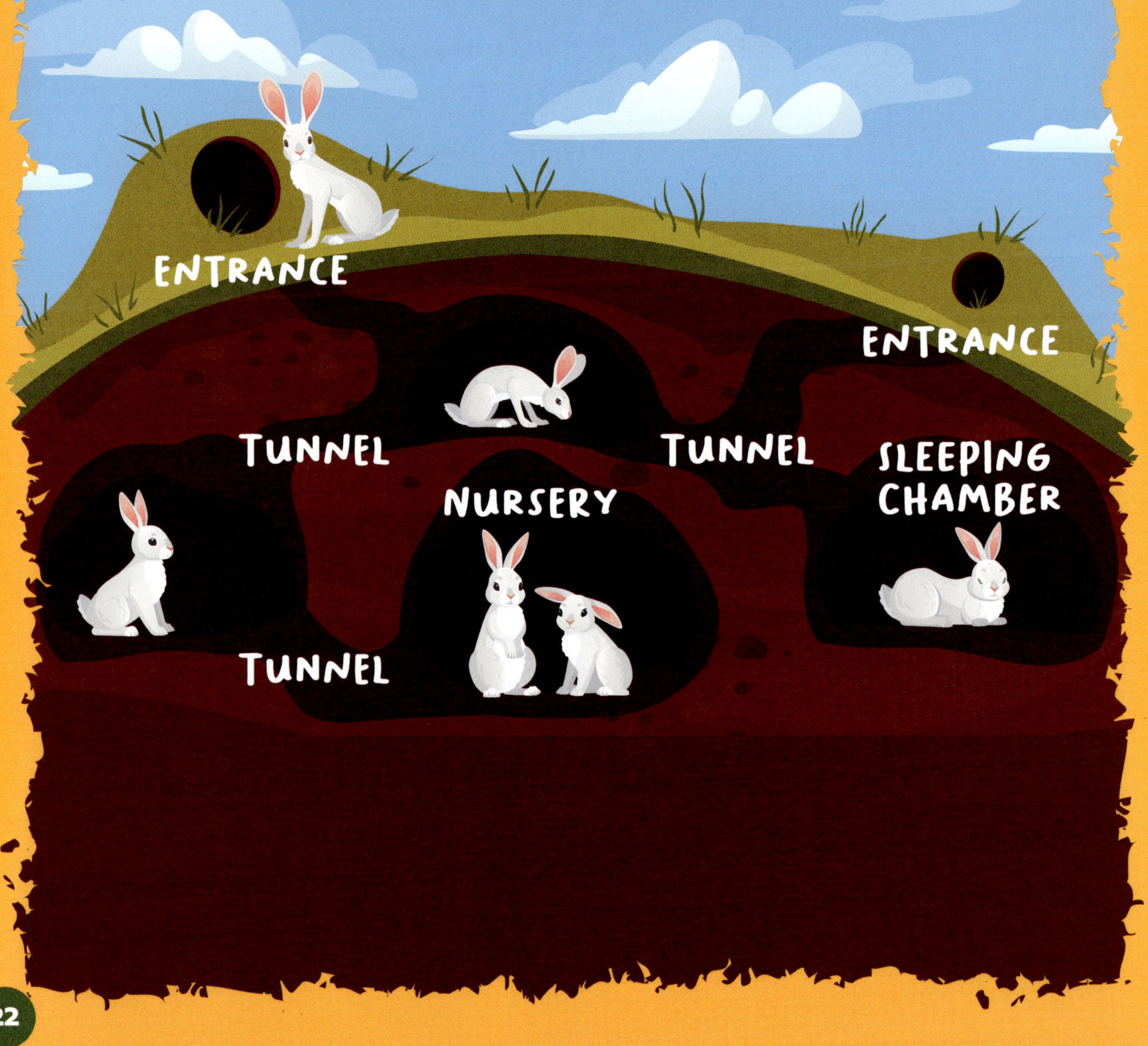

GLOSSARY

burrow (bur-oh) a tunnel or hole in the ground used by an animal

chambers (chaym-burz) rooms

colony (kah-luh-nee) a large group of animals that live together

dominant (dah-muh-nuhnt) most powerful or in charge

nursery (nur-sur-ee) a place to raise babies

predators (pred-uh-turz) animals that live by hunting other animals for food

shallow (shal-oh) not deep

territory (ter-i-tor-ee) an area of land under control by a group

FURTHER READING

Denega, Danielle. *A Colony of Rabbits.* Children's Press, 2023.

McDonald, Amy. *Rabbits.* Bellwether Media, 2021.

ON THE INTERNET

10 Hopping Fun Rabbit Facts!
www.natgeokids.com/uk/discover/animals/general-animals/10-hopping-fun-rabbit-facts/
National Geographic Kids shares their favorite facts about rabbits.

Rabbit and Hare
https://kids.britannica.com/kids/article/rabbit-and-hare/353689
Learn about different kinds of rabbits and where they live with Britannica Kids.

INDEX